A STUDY GUIDE FOR COMMON SENSE POLICE SUPERVISION

A Study Guide for

COMMON SENSE POLICE SUPERVISION

Practical Tips for the First-Line Leader

Seventh Edition

By

GERALD W. GARNER

Chief of Police
Corinth Police Department
Corinth, Texas

CHARLES C THOMAS • PUBLISHER, LTD.
Springfield • Illinois • USA

Published and Distributed Throughout the World by

CHARLES C THOMAS • PUBLISHER, LTD.
2600 South First Street
Springfield, Illinois 62704

© 2024 by CHARLES C THOMAS • PUBLISHER, LTD.

ISBN 978-0-398-09448-5 (paper)
ISBN 978-0-398-09449-2 (ebook)

With THOMAS BOOKS *careful attention is given to all details of manufacturing and design. It is the Publisher's desire to present books that are satisfactory as to their physical qualities and artistic possibilities and appropriate for their particular use. Thomas Books will be true to those laws of quality that assure a good name and good will.*

Printed in the United States of America
CM-C-1

PREFACE

This comprehensive study guide is intended to be a companion for the Seventh Edition of *Common Sense Police Supervision*. it was developed to help readers and students test their knowledge of the contents of the nineteen chapter text. It also was fashioned to help the promotional student ready himself for an examination based on the book.

A summary of the contents of each chapter is provided at the beginning of each of this guide's nineteen sections. The summary is followed by a series of questions designed to test and reinforce the reader's knowledge and understanding of the chapter. Each of the guide's questions is of the multiple-choice variety. The reader should select the single best response to answer the question or complete the sentence correctly. There will be only one entirely correct answer for each question. The correct answer to each question follows in a separate section. The number of the page from which the answer was taken is also provided as an additional learning tool.

This guide will not replace a thorough and careful reading (and rereading) of the book, *Common Sense Police Supervision*. However, if used along with the book, it should increase the reader's comprehension and retention of the material found in the text.

CONTENTS

A STUDY GUIDE FOR COMMON SENSE POLICE SUPERVISION

Chapter 1

WHAT IS SUPERVISION?

SUMMARY

Supervision means a lot of things to a lot of people. If he is to supervise effectively, a police leader will have to serve as a trainer, planner, disciplinarian, counselor, listener, confidant, communicator, performance evaluator and a number of other things. He will be a manager, too, and move ideas and information up and down the chain of command.

The police supervisor will find his work more challenging than will most first-line leaders outside of law enforcement. The police leader already knows that this profession is something different and apart, and so are the people who labor in it. The police supervisor will find many of his subordinates espousing a strong sense of justice and belief in a just cause. Those are assets the supervisor very likely shares with his people and can build upon to the benefit of his agency and the citizens they all serve.

Supervision in law enforcement is indeed, in many ways, different. It requires a special sort of individual to do it well.

QUESTIONS

1. Common sense entails the practical application of _____.

   a. Good judgment
   b. Prudence
   c. Aptitude for calm and logical reasoning
   d. All of the above

2. In the case of the police employee, work product is delivered in the form of _____.

   a. Traffic enforcement
   b. Quality arrests
   c. Police service
   d. Written reports

3. Today's police supervisor will be a _____.

   a. Planner
   b. Trainer and educator
   c. Counselor
   d. All of the above

4. The good police supervisor will excel in the concise use of _____ as tools.

   a. Meanings
   b. Words
   c. Force
   d. None of the above

5. As a performance evaluator, the supervisor will report _____.

   a. Facts
   b. Assumptions
   c. Allegations
   d. Suppositions

6. The police supervisor will serve as a _____ role model for correct and moral behavior, on-duty and off-duty.

   a. Flawless
   b. Neutral
   c. Negative
   d. Positive

7. Many law enforcement officers are _____.

   a. Constructively suspicious
   b. Mildly cynical
   c. Somewhat egotistical
   d. All of the above

8. The police sergeant is responsible for translating his department's policies, rules and regulations into _____.

   a. Statistical productivity
   b. Adequate probable cause
   c. Ample probable cause
   d. On-the-job compliance

9. A supervisor must move _____ up and down the chain of command.

   a. Discipline
   b. Complaints
   c. Information
   d. Grievances

10. The police supervisor will find that many of his subordinates espouse a strong sense of _____.

    a. Justice
    b. Courtesy
    c. Legal knowledge
    d. All of the above

11. First of all, the supervisor is expected to _____.

    a. Challenge
    b. Speak up
    c. Lead
    d. Obey the rules

12. The supervisor's most important role is that of a positive _____.

    a. Manager
    b. Public speaker
    c. Role model
    d. Public advocate

13. The supervisor's disciplinary efforts should be directed primarily at _____.

    a. Punishment
    b. Changed behavior
    c. Improved performance
    d. Both b and c

14. A good supervisor will excel in the concise use of _____ as tools.

    a. Statistics
    b. Words
    c. Numbers
    d. None of the above

15. Law enforcement supervision is much more about _____ than theory.

    a. Precedent
    b. Legal precedent
    c. Practical application
    d. None of the above

16. Effective supervision requires _____ and practical skills.

    a. Common sense
    b. Minimal inspection
    c. Micromanagement
    d. All of the above

17. Many of the challenges a police supervisor faces are _____ unique to the law enforcement profession.

    a. Not
    b. Always
    c. Usually
    d. None of the above

18. A police supervisor is responsible for _____ broad guidelines into on-the-job compliance by his subordinates.

    a. Filtering
    b. Translating
    c. Altering
    d. Revising

19. The police officer of several years' experience is often increasingly _____ in his approach to life.

    a. Cynical
    b. Distrusting
    c. Violent
    d. Both a and b

20. The police leader will have to furnish _____ rewards for the officer who gets few thanks from a public that may understand very little about his job.

    a. Financial
    b. Monetary
    c. Mental
    d. Spiritual

ANSWERS

1. D., 5

2. C., 6

3. D., 6–7

4. B., 8

5. A., 9

6. D., 13

7. D., 14

8. D., 16

9. C., 18

10. A., 11

11. C., 6

12. C., 18

13. D., 7

14. B., 8

15. C., 4

16. A., 18

17. A., 19

18. B., 16

19. D., 14

20. C., 13

Chapter 2

PREPARATION FOR THE ROLE
OF POLICE SUPERVISOR

SUMMARY

The upwardly mobile police officer must alter a bit the way he thinks, feels and acts. As a supervisor, he will have to see the big picture, not a fragment of a snapshot of the total scene. His relations with his old peers will change, as will his associations with management.

The would-be police supervisor must prepare mentally for the change in outlook that he will face if promoted. In seeking that promotion, he must master the knowledge of his profession, including pertinent statutes, case law, rules and regulations, policies and procedures and supervisory principles. He must hone his test-taking skills and practice his presentations for an oral board or assessment center. He must remain mindful that appearance, demeanor, and sincerity will go a long way towards figuring his final score in the promotional process. Most of all, he must remember to be himself and respond thoughtfully, courageously, and honestly to the tests and trials of promotion. That is the best preparation of all.

QUESTIONS

1. _____ alone is probably not the best of reasons for wanting a promotion.

   a. Pride
   b. Rank
   c. Money
   d. Prestige

2. _____ can be the strongest of motivations.

   a. Money
   b. Prestige
   c. Pride
   d. Peer pressure

3. The process of personnel review and evaluation must be carried out _____ in the successful police organization.

   a. Continuously
   b. Sporadically
   c. Irregularly
   d. Occasionally

4. Discipline is a process in which the supervisor must demonstrate_____ and support.

   a. Participation
   b. Discussion
   c. Opposition
   d. Assessment

5. The officer who has great difficulty expressing himself in written format will have _____ obstacles to overcome as a supervisor.

   a. Few
   b. Minor
   c. Moderate
   d. Serious

6. Becoming involved in the difficulties of subordinates, sometimes at a very sensitive level, is a/an _____ part of a supervisor's role as counselor.

    a. Unpleasant
    b. Distasteful
    c. Unnecessary
    d. Necessary

7. A good candidate for a supervisor's slot must demonstrate that he has acquired _____ job skills.

    a. Technical
    b. Wide-ranging
    c. Sensitive
    d. Singular

8. _____ about any test can be dangerous for the test-taker.

    a. Self-confidence
    b. Self-assuredness
    c. Assumptions
    d. Doubts

9. In test taking, a common mistake to be avoided is _____.

    a. Cheating
    b. Spending too much time on a single question
    c. Spending too little time on a single question
    d. Thinking too much

10. Which of the following exercises might be found in a promotional assessment center?

    a. Role playing exercise
    b. Oral presentation
    c. Impromptu speaking
    d. All of the above exercises

11. Which of the following exercises might be found in a promotional assessment center?

    a. Tactical scenario
    b. In-basket exercise
    c. Writing assignment(s)
    d. All of the above exercises

12. During a promotional interview the candidate should be _____.

    a. Subservient
    b. Ramrod-stiff
    c. Self-depreciating
    d. None of the above

13. The jump to supervisor begins with careful and thoughtful _____ for promotional consideration and competition.

    a. Preparations
    b. Discussions
    c. Career planning
    d. None of the above

14. The would-be police supervisor must prepare _____ for the change in outlook that he will face if promoted.

    a. Gradually
    b. Mentally
    c. Hypothetically
    d. All of the above

15. Not everyone is _____ suited to be a supervisor.

    a. Physically
    b. Politically
    c. Emotionally
    d. Naturally

16. The jump from first-line employee to first-line supervisor is the _____ leap in law enforcement.

    a. Biggest
    b. Easiest
    c. Strangest
    d. Shortest

17. Most of all, the supervisory promotional candidate must remember to be _____ and respond thoughtfully, courageously and honestly to the tests and trials of promotion.

    a. Subservient
    b. Himself
    c. Both a and b
    d. Neither a nor b

18. To do the job of personnel evaluation properly, the supervisor must above all else be _____ and sincere.

    a. Empathetic
    b. Sympathetic
    c. Condescending
    d. Frank

19. Employee grievances against the agency and its supervisors require an extreme amount of supervisory _____.

    a. Patience
    b. Fairness
    c. Integrity
    d. All of the above

20. The wise promotional candidate will practice talking intelligently about _____.

    a. Himself
    b. His department
    c. His supervisor
    d. His family

ANSWERS

1. C., 20

2. D., 20

3. A., 22

4. A., 23

5. D., 23

6. D., 25

7. B., 27

8. C., 32

9. B., 33

10. D., 35

11. D., 35–36

12. D., 39

13. A., 40

14. B., 41

15. C., 42

16. A., 42

17. B., 41

18. D., 23

19. D., 24

20. A., 34

Chapter 3

ETHICS OF POLICE SUPERVISION

SUMMARY

The supervisor who wants to do his job well is responsible and accountable to the citizens he serves, whatever his jurisdiction happens to be. He owes them the best service he can render. The supervisor owes a certain debt of responsibility to the profession of policing itself. He owes that profession the most ethical, responsible, competent job he can do.

Most of all, the police leader laboring persistently and ethically within the guidelines of his responsibilities must recognize his paramount obligation to himself. There is no one he should less want to disappoint. He must, in the end, satisfy himself and his own image of what he wants to be. If his actions please others, that's great. If his boss is happy about his performance, that is an added bonus.

Only when the supervisor knows that he is performing in a manner in which he can be rightfully and personally proud can he honestly claim to be meeting the ethical requisites of his calling.

QUESTIONS

1. Ethics are said to deal with the nature of the _____.

   a. "Right and wrong"
   b. "Good and right"
   c. "Fair and unfair"
   d. None of the above

2. The Police Supervisor's Code of Ethics deals primarily with the issue of _____.

   a. Fairness
   b. Justice
   c. Courage
   d. Loyalty

3. The Police Supervisor's Code of Ethics also deals with the issue of _____.

   a. Human frailties
   b. Exceptions
   c. Frequent lapses
   d. Extraordinary events

4. The intelligent supervisor will ask for _____ of orders or policies that he does not understand.

   a. Reversal
   b. Reconsideration
   c. Temporary suspension
   d. Clarification

5. The ethical police supervisor must develop a reputation for _____ with his superiors.

   a. Toughness
   b. Mental toughness
   c. Empathy
   d. Reliability

6. One of the first-line supervisor's key responsibilities is _____.

    a. Detecting untruths
    b. The gathering and reporting of facts
    c. Mental toughness
    d. Sincere subservience

7. An earned reputation for a lack of _____ on the part of the supervisor will lessen his value to the agency.

    a. Toughness
    b. Credibility
    c. Subservience
    d. Mental toughness

8. The responsible police supervisor confronts the fostering and spread of _____.

    a. War stories
    b. Rumors
    c. Badge Bunnies
    d. Criticism

9. The supervisor who cannot work and _____ well with his peers is not fulfilling his responsibility to his employer or to himself.

    a. Play
    b. Communicate
    c. Debate
    d. Argue

10. The supervisor is his employees' link with higher authority and he must accurately relay or transmit what to the levels of the organization where it/they can be acted upon?

    a. Their grievances
    b. Their thoughts
    c. Their feelings
    d. All of the above

11. The responsible supervisor will show _____ for his subordinates' problems and worries.

    a. Limited sympathy
    b. Limited empathy
    c. Genuine concern
    d. None of the above

12. Loyalty and responsibility to one's employees requires hard work and _____ on the part of the police supervisor.

    a. Occasionally turning a blind eye
    b. Tolerance
    c. Sound character
    d. Forgiveness

13. The effective police supervisor's enthusiasm and devotion for his job can inspire _____ in his team.

    a. Imitation
    b. Resentment
    c. Opposition
    d. Confusion

14. It is the supervisor's task to assure that he and his people produce results that may be _____ of what the public expects of "government employees."

    a. Typical
    b. Atypical
    c. Supportive
    d. Unsupportive

15. The police leader knows that he and his people labor in an environment that presents the opportunity for _____ behavior.

    a. Unethical
    b. Improper
    c. Illegal
    d. All of the above

16. By living his personal life in a/an _____ way, the ethical law enforcement leader denies the rumor mongers the ammunition to destroy him and his agency.

    a. Secretive
    b. Confidential
    c. Moral
    d. Amoral

17. The good police supervisor owes his profession the most _____ job he can possibly do.

    a. Ethical
    b. Responsible
    c. Competent
    d. All of the above

18. The ethical law enforcement leader knows that he best serves his community as well as his subordinates when he acts as a _____ for what a peace officer should be.

    a. Symbol of authority
    b. Positive role model
    c. Paragon of virtue
    d. None of the above

19. The supervisor who is loyal to his superiors sees to it that he follows the _____ and requires his subordinates to do the same.

    a. Informal chain of command
    b. Existing chain of command
    c. Line of least resistance
    d. None of the above

20. The leader has obligations to himself and assures that he or she remains _____ healthy.

    a. Physically
    b. Emotionally
    c. Morally
    d. All of the above

ANSWERS

1. B., 43

2. D., 44

3. A., 44

4. D., 45

5. D., 46

6. B., 46–47

7. B., 48

8. B., 50

9. B., 49

10. D., 51

11. C., 53

12. C., 56

13. A., 58

14. B., 59

15. D., 59

16. C., 60

17. D., 60

18. B., 60

19. B., 50

20. D., 61

Chapter 4

QUALITIES OF A LEADER

SUMMARY

The chapter presented a virtual laundry list of what being a supervisor requires of the would-be leader. As a leader, the police supervisor will have many and diverse tasks, none of which is more vital than his obligation to prepare his subordinates for their work. He will strive to accomplish this preparation through adequate and continuing education and training.

QUESTIONS

1. The theory that leaders are born and not made describes the
   _____ leader.

   a. Formal
   b. Born
   c. Natural
   d. Humanistic

2. An effective law enforcement leader should exhibit which trait(s)?

   a. Integrity
   b. Personal courage
   c. Loyalty
   d. All of the above

3. An effective law enforcement leader should exhibit which additional traits(s)?

   a. Vision
   b. Common sense
   c. Truthfulness
   d. All of the above

4. An effective law enforcement leader should exhibit which trait(s)?

   a. Tact
   b. Trust
   c. Fairness
   d. All of the above

5. Some known bar(s) or obstacle(s) to effective leadership include
   _____.

   a. Frequent displays of temper to subordinates
   b. Playing favorites with subordinates
   c. Holding a grudge or getting even with subordinates
   d. All of the above

6. Some additional bar(s) or obstacles to effective leadership include
   _____.

   a. Distorting the truth with lies or intentional omissions
   b. Setting a poor example
   c. Showing no loyalty to anything or anyone
   d. All of the above

7. Command presence in the police supervisor should include _____.

   a. Self-assertiveness
   b. Ramrod-stiff backbone
   c. Rigid personality
   d. Aggression

8. Command presence includes _____.

   a. An expression of absolute peace
   b. Avoiding difficult decision-making
   c. The ability to appear in control of oneself
   d. Persistent anger

9. The most valuable asset(s) of the police supervisor include(s)
   _____.

   a. Calmness
   b. Self-confidence
   c. Self-control
   d. All of the above

10. Command speaks of _____.

    a. Indecisiveness
    b. Timidity
    c. Confidence
    d. None of the above

11. A sense of well-being, sometimes referred to as good morale, can come from working for a supervisor who _____.

    a. Sets reasonable objectives
    b. Lets subordinates know what the objectives are
    c. Leads the subordinates in reaching for success
    d. All of the above

12. A good supervisor will help prepare his subordinates for their work by _____.

    a. Micromanaging them at all times
    b. Assuring that they receive adequate education and training
    c. Providing them with *laissez-faire* supervision at all times
    d. All of the above

13. The best leaders display ample command presence without appearing _____.

    a. Arrogant
    b. Competent
    c. Empathetic
    d. Loyal

14. The subordinates of a strong and effective leader are more likely to display _____ than are the subordinates of a poor leader.

    a. Indecisiveness
    b. Low morale
    c. High morale
    d. Lack of self-confidence

15. _____ are among the most important traits that a law enforcement leader can demonstrate.

    a. Indecisiveness and timidity
    b. Arrogance and anger
    c. Integrity and personal courage
    d. None of the above

16. Holding grudges and seeking revenge against others will _____ the leader's effectiveness.

    a. Sabotage
    b. Enhance
    c. Bolster
    d. Emphasize

17. It is obvious that proper _____ behavior is a must for a successful police supervisor.

    a. Legal
    b. Moral
    c. Ethical
    d. All of the above

18. _____ means doing the right things for the right reasons even (or especially) when no one is watching.

    a. Credibility
    b. Truthfulness
    c. Integrity
    d. Faith

19. A lack of _____ or follow-through on the part of his subordinate leaders often tops the list of the CEO's complaints.

    a. Credibility
    b. Reliability
    c. Honesty
    d. Truthfulness

20. The supervisor should seldom encounter situations requiring public, immediate and summary _____ of his personnel.

    a. Praise
    b. Tail-chewing
    c. Commendation
    d. Constructive criticism

ANSWERS

1. C., 62

2. D., 63–65

3. D., 65–67

4. D., 69–71

5. D., 72–75

6. D., 76–78

7. A., 81

8. C., 81

9. D., 82

10. C., 82

11. D., 83

12. B., 83

13. A., 85

14. C., 85

15. C., 84

16. A., 84

17. D., 63

18. C., 64

19. B., 68

20. B., 73

Chapter 5

THE POLICE LEADER AS AN EDUCATOR

SUMMARY

In his role as a facilitator of learning, the police leader assesses his employees' training needs and then works to help them meet those needs. If he is fortunate, he may find skilled instructors on needed topics inside or outside the agency to handle the teaching chores. If not, he may need to handle the task himself.

The effective instructor utilizes a carefully prepared lesson plan, complete with identifiable learning objectives that can be measured to help guide him in his work. Likewise, he uses demonstrations, class participation, field exercises, and learning aids such as video presentations to get the message across. Finally, he questions, talks with, and observes his student officers after the training is given to see if the desired results have been attained. In doing so he recognizes that the learning process for a law enforcement professional never ends.

The smart supervisor also recognizes the great value to be found in on-line training courses. One of the assets of this kind of instruction is that it permits the student to proceed at his or her own pace.

QUESTIONS

1. The police supervisor should be a(n) _____ part of the training or instructional effort.

   a. Occasional
   b. Backup
   c. Integral
   d. None of the above

2. Which topic(s) is/are likely to be included in topics for police instruction?

   a. Firearms policy and firearms use
   b. Handling of the mentally ill
   c. Interviewing skills
   d. All of the above

3. An effective police supervisor will _____ his subordinates' training needs and help obtain that training for them.

   a. Assess
   b. Collate
   c. Collect
   d. All of the above

4. In order to best perform his duties as a competent trainer of peace officers the supervisor will need to know _____.

   a. How to organize what he is going to teach
   b. Which instructional method he is going to use
   c. How he will evaluate the results on his "students"
   d. All of the above

5. Good instructors put together a/an _____ before they commence their teaching efforts in front of a class.

   a. PowerPoint presentation
   b. Slide show
   c. Lesson plan
   d. None of the above

6. An effective lesson plan's aim is to _____.

   a. Provide instructor and instructed with an idea of what is to be accomplished
   b. Describe how it is to be done
   c. Describe how the student will show that he has mastered the material
   d. All of the above

7. An effective lesson plan often contains _____.

   a. Overview
   b. Objectives
   c. Outline and/or notes
   d. All of the above

8. Which of the following is/are a valid means for evaluating whether or not the police "student" learned the material presented?

   a. Written test
   b. Oral test
   c. Observation of performance
   d. All of the above

9. Which form(s) of teaching presentation may be the least successful if used alone in front of today's generation of students?

   a. Discussion
   b. Demonstration
   c. Lecture
   d. Participation

10. Students should be permitted to _____ their instructors.

   a. Evaluate
   b. Oppose
   c. Support
   d. Label

11. Which is a criticism sometimes heard from students regarding their instructor?

    a. The instructor talked too fast
    b. The instructor did not know his subject
    c. The instructor appeared bored or uninterested
    d. All of the above

12. "Because I say so" is generally considered a _____ response from the instructor in a classroom setting.

    a. Shallow and unacceptable
    b. Adequate and acceptable
    c. Correct and appropriate
    d. None of the above

13. A lawsuit alleging _____ may follow a bad shooting by officers.

    a. Insubordination
    b. Use of force
    c. Failure to train
    d. None of the above

14. In his role as a facilitator of learning, the police leader _____.

    a. Refers training needs to the agency head
    b. Assesses his employees' training needs
    c. Refers training needs to the HR department
    d. None of the above

15. The effective instructor utilizes a carefully prepared lesson plan, complete with identifiable learning objectives that can be _____ to help guide him in his work.

    a. Minimized
    b. Maximized
    c. Measured
    d. All of the above

16. A good training lesson plan includes an overview, objectives, out-
    line, evaluation, and _____ section.

    a. Conclusions
    b. Sources
    c. Summary
    d. Executive summary

17. The lesson plan's _____ presents a short summation of what
    the supervisor-instructor hopes to accomplish with the lesson.

    a. Evaluation
    b. Outline
    c. Overview
    d. Conclusion

18. The lesson plan's _____ should list the specific skills or knowl-
    edge that will be imparted in order to attain the aims of the goal.

    a. Objectives
    b. Overview
    c. Summary
    d. Sources

19. The _____ has one advantage. It conveys a volume of factual
    knowledge in a no-nonsense fashion in minimal time.

    a. Discussion
    b. Demonstration
    c. Lecture
    d. None of the above

20. Which question(s) might be found on a student's evaluation form
    to be completed on his instructor?

    a. Did the instructor hold your attention?
    b. How could this presentation be improved?
    c. Did the instructor appear interested in his subject?
    d. All of the above

ANSWERS

1. C., 87

2. D., 88–89

3. A., 90

4. D., 92

5. C., 91

6. D., 92

7. D., 92

8. D., 94

9. C., 97

10. A., 99–100

11. D., 100–101

12. A., 103

13. C., 102

14. B., 104

15. C., 104

16. B., 104

17. C., 92

18. A., 92

19. C., 97

20. D., 99–100

Chapter 6

THE POLICE LEADER AS AN EVALUATOR

SUMMARY

The police supervisor's job as an evaluator is a multifaceted one. He must be a keen observer, a fair and accurate reporter, and a patient and tactful leader. He must, in the final analysis, be one who effectively rates, records, and where necessary, requires improvements in the efforts of his police subordinates.

As an impartial and accurate evaluator the supervisor will furnish hard evidence and examples to back his opinions. He will stay focused on the subject at hand, assure completeness of the assessment and emphasize its importance by getting it done on time. Then, he will follow up the performance appraisal session with inspections and observations as required. If indicated, he will apply appropriate rewards and sanctions. The wise supervisor realizes that his or her job as an evaluator is a never-ending one.

QUESTIONS

1. Properly administered and closely monitored by command staff as well as _____ the performance appraisal system can identify problems in the department's selection, training or operational procedures.

    a. Citizens
    b. The public
    c. Line supervisors
    d. All of the above

2. _____, not just people, can be evaluated and strengthened through a good evaluation system.

    a. Discipline
    b. Character
    c. Procedures
    d. None of the above

3. Which police employees should have their job performance evaluated periodically?

    a. All police employees
    b. Sworn police employees
    c. Civilian police employees
    d. All police employees except command staff

4. In regards to law enforcement employee performance evaluations, the agency's leaders must first decide what is to be _____.

    a. Listed
    b. Measured
    c. Estimated
    d. Approximated

5. It is vital that performance appraisals only look at behavior or results that is/are _____.

 a. Tangible
 b. Observable
 c. Capable of being measured in some way
 d. All of the above

6. Results can be measured; _____ cannot.

 a. Attitudes
 b. Outcome
 c. Productivity
 d. Output

7. Which of the following is/are general job knowledge and skills that are often measured in a performance review or evaluation of a law enforcement officer?

 a. Interviewing skills
 b. Report writing
 c. Knowledge of the area
 d. All of the above

8. Which of the following is/are personal characteristics that are often measured in a performance review or evaluation of a law enforcement officer?

 a. Handling of stress
 b. Judgment
 c. Self-confidence
 d. All of the above

9. The format chosen for an employee job performance evaluation should be relatively _____ throughout the agency.

 a. Varied
 b. Uniform
 c. Differentiated
 d. Inconsistent

10. What is the primary disadvantage or drawback of the "open narrative" written evaluation?

    a. Takes too much time
    b. Takes too much effort
    c. Inability of some supervisors to write well
    d. None of the above

11. A finished evaluation should be _____ carefully at least twice by its writer.

    a. Revised
    b. Reworded
    c. Proofread
    d. Shortened

12. The supervisor-rater preparing a fair and effective performance evaluation will take which of the following steps?

    a. Furnish evidence or backing for all evaluation statements
    b. Not spring any surprises
    c. Be fair and accurate
    d. All of the above

13. Which of the following word choices is/are generally considered unacceptable and inappropriate for the supervisor to use during an evaluation discussion with a subordinate?

    a. Reckless
    b. Punctual
    c. Imprecise
    d. None of the above

14. In preparing an evaluation, precise statements and examples are preferable to _____ remarks.

    a. Specific
    b. Generalized
    c. Specified
    d. Truthful

15. A good evaluation should not _____ statistics.

    a. Include
    b. Omit
    c. Summarize
    d. Overemphasize

16. Quotas and rigid targets set in numbers are _____ yardsticks when used alone for evaluative purposes.

    a. Poor
    b. Excellent
    c. Good
    d. Appropriate

17. Ideally, evaluations should in no way be tied to _____ pay.

    a. Increased
    b. Bonus
    c. Longevity
    d. Merit

18. Bonuses or other performance incentives arising out of good evaluation reports should reflect truly _____ work.

    a. Average
    b. Below average
    c. Extraordinary
    d. None of the above

19. What is the required number of goals and objectives to be listed in a well-written employee evaluation?

    a. Three
    b. Four
    c. Extraordinary
    d. None of the above

20. Every police agency should have some kind of a _____ to recognize extraordinary job performance of employees at all levels and assignments in the organization.

  a. Punishment system
  b. Reward system
  c. Appeal system
  d. Graduated system

ANSWERS

1. C., 108

2. C., 108

3. A., 109

4. B., 109

5. D., 109

6. A., 109

7. D., 111

8. D., 112

9. B., 113

10. C., 115–116

11. C., 117

12. D., 117–119

13. A., 119

14. B., 120

15. D., 121

16. A., 121

17. C., 121

18. C., 122

19. D., 129

20. B., 130

Chapter 7

THE POLICE LEADER AS A DISCIPLINARIAN

SUMMARY

The police supervisor's role is a key one. He MUST be involved in the disciplinary process. Allowing him to meet his full potential boosts the organization as a whole and its employees and leaders as individuals. It is the first line supervisor's responsibility to guarantee that he meets his obligations through a judicious application of fairness, intelligence, job skills, and plain common sense.

QUESTIONS

1. Discipline involves correction and allows for a _____ change in behavior.

   a. Sudden
   b. Gradual
   c. Beneficial
   d. Negative

2. Discipline as it pertains to police work might be described as training and preparation that help develop _____ in the police employee.

   a. Self-control
   b. Sound character
   c. Job efficiency
   d. All of the above

3. Discipline can be described as a/an _____.

   a. Attitude
   b. Condition
   c. Set of rules
   d. Set of orders

4. When a disciplined attitude is lacking, _____ in another of its forms will be necessary.

   a. Punishment
   b. Morale
   c. Discipline
   d. Recognition

5. Corrective action selected by a supervisor must fit the known _____ of circumstances.

   a. Summary
   b. Conclusion
   c. Totality
   d. Collection

6. Too _____ a corrective response may embitter the employee and destroy the morale of his coworkers.

    a. Sudden
    b. Harsh
    c. Direct
    d. None of the above

7. _____ aimed at the supervisor may be the result of an initial confrontation with a victim of alcoholism.

    a. Anger
    b. Denial
    c. Direct
    d. a. and b.

8. The Americans with Disabilities Act (ADA) _____ a supervisor from acting immediately when he has cause to believe he is dealing with an under the influence police employee.

    a. Prohibits
    b. Does not prohibit
    c. Delays
    d. Cautions

9. Problems in employee behavior must be _____ to help and protect the employee and his fellow workers.

    a. Lessened
    b. Deferred
    c. Corrected
    d. Disclosed

10. In order to be effective, reward/punishment must be _____ enough for the person being rewarded/punished to connect his actions with the results.

    a. Sure
    b. Immediate
    c. Both a and b
    d. Neither a nor b

11. Corrective action, to be accepted as fair and just by the party on the receiving end, must be _____ with what has gone before.

    a. Identical
    b. Consistent
    c. Concurrent
    d. Consecutive

12. When identical or similar infractions earn identical or similar penalties it is known as _____ discipline.

    a. Progressive
    b. Comparative
    c. Negative
    d. Positive

13. Under the concept of _____ discipline, more severe penalties are imposed for repeated improper behavior on the part of the employee.

    a. Progressive
    b. Comparative
    c. Negative
    d. Positive

14. _____ in determining appropriate discipline must remain available to the supervisor for the out of the ordinary situation.

    a. Support
    b. Forgiveness
    c. Leeway
    d. Consistency

15. To be effective, corrective action must be _____ to determine if a change in behavior or performance actually results.

    a. Confirmed
    b. Severe
    c. Strengthened
    d. Followed up

16. Corrective action, in order to be most efficient, must be _____.

    a. Timely
    b. Fair
    c. Documented
    d. All of the above

17. Which is a basic commandment the supervisor must adhere to in executing corrective action of any sort?

    a. Have the necessary information and know the whole story
    b. Have the required official support before taking corrective action
    c. Massive doses of authority should be avoided whenever possible
    d. All of the above

18. Having the primary supervisor thoroughly involved in the corrective process accomplishes what?

    a. Correction is personalized for the employee
    b. Correction is appropriate
    c. Participation in correction strengthens the supervisor
    d. All of the above

19. The supervisor must make sure that any disciplinary action he takes is done _____.

    a. By the book
    b. According to existing department procedures
    c. Both a and b
    d. Neither a nor b

20. _____ is the highest level of discipline.

    a. Positive discipline
    b. Self-discipline
    c. Negative discipline
    d. Progressive discipline

ANSWERS

1. C., 132

2. D., 132

3. A., 132

4. C., 133

5. C., 134

6. B., 135

7. D., 136

8. B., 137

9. C., 139

10. C., 139

11. B., 141

12. B., 141

13. A., 141

14. C., 141

15. D., 142

16. D., 143

17. D., 144–145

18. D., 146–147

19. C., 147

20. B., 148

Chapter 8

THE POLICE LEADER AS A PLANNER

SUMMARY

The police supervisor must be an effective planner at several levels. He is careful to craft specific, tangible, clear objectives that focus on results. As a planner, the supervisor helps subordinates formulate their job-related goals and objectives. In doing so, he helps them learn to plan well for themselves. In addition, the capable supervisor plans how he will execute a project or assignment for his boss.

The wise supervisor plans for himself, too. Here he does more than plan for the operations of the work day, week, or month, as important as those plans may be. He also will plan for his future in law enforcement. He knows that with a carefully thought out action plan for the future, he can demonstrate his greatest value to the police organization as he maximizes his own advancement and personal job satisfaction within the agency. That is called planning for success.

The supervisor/planner with more than his share of common sense recognizes that he is of not much use to anyone if he does not also take care of his own personal and professional planning. It is when he plans carefully and wisely for himself that he can continue to be of the most use to others.

QUESTIONS

1. _____ plays a large and critical role in police work.

   a. Use of force
   b. Planning
   c. Use of lethal force
   d. Use of minimal force

2. The act of _____ is referred to as the preparation of some sort of scheme, design, or manner of operating, to achieve some end goal or objective.

   a. Prevarication
   b. Performance review
   c. Planning
   d. Performance evaluation

3. If the planning task is to be a long one, perhaps covering weeks or months of work time, a/an _____ will be helpful to the supervisor.

   a. Timetable or schedule
   b. Plan
   c. Outline
   d. Assistant

4. _____ of a proposed plan is vital.

   a. Reconsideration
   b. Reversal
   c. Cancellation
   d. Discussion

5. The advice of _____ is critical to the eventual success of any plan.

   a. Critics
   b. Critical thinkers
   c. Fellow supervisors
   d. Elected officials

6. A planning schedule should be as _____ as possible.

    a. Fixed
    b. Rigid
    c. Inflexible
    d. Flexible

7. Failure to make _____ changes in a plan indicates a lack of good judgment.

    a. Rapid
    b. Gradual
    c. Needed
    d. Inflexible

8. Once the plan has been refined, clarified, and altered to the satisfaction of the supervisor-planner, the next step calls for _____ the plan's elements to those who will enact it.

    a. Summarizing
    b. Outlining
    c. Communicating
    d. Emphasizing

9. In planning, there is no limit on the number of _____ that may be prepared on the way to the final product.

    a. Arguments
    b. Rough drafts
    c. Corrections
    d. Conclusions

10. Which is a characteristic of an effective, successful planning objective?

    a. Good planning objectives are specific.
    b. Good planning objectives are tangible.
    c. Good planning objectives focus on results.
    d. All of the above

11. Which is an additional characteristic of an effective, successful planning objective?

    a. Good planning objectives are significant.
    b. Good planning objectives are clear.
    c. Good planning objectives are challenging but not idealistic.
    d. All of the above

12. Occasionally, the police supervisor may be required to set an employee planning objective without the subordinate's _____.

    a. Knowledge
    b. Concurrence
    c. Information
    d. Realization

13. Which is a simple yet valid guideline for planning employee goals and objectives?

    a. The objective should be specific, concise and to the point.
    b. Planning objectives should include a deadline for accomplishment.
    c. Only objectives that are beneficial to both the employee and the police agency should be used.
    d. All of the above

14. A good, written employee planning objective generally utilizes action-oriented _____.

    a. Adverbs
    b. Adjectives
    c. Verbs
    d. All of the above

15. When engaging in a planning project for his boss, the police supervisor must have a crystal clear _____ of what is expected of him.

    a. Outline
    b. Understanding
    c. Summary
    d. Conclusion

16. The wise supervisor will examine his plan carefully for errors and
_____.

   a. Opinions
   b. Conclusions
   c. Omissions
   d. None of the above

17. _____ skills are to be found in every effective supervisor's tool
box.

   a. Timekeeping
   b. Timeliness
   c. Time out
   d. Time management

18. The police supervisor should be _____ in the career plan that he
sets for himself.

   a. Optimistic
   b. Pessimistic
   c. Realistic
   d. Hopeful

19. The police supervisor must be an effective _____ at several levels.

   a. Debater
   b. Oracle
   c. Planner
   d. Plotter

20. Planning goals for employee performance should, where possible,
be done with _____ from the employee.

   a. Opposition
   b. Argument
   c. Disagreement
   d. Input

ANSWERS

1. B., 149

2. C., 149

3. A., 151

4. D., 151

5. C., 151

6. D., 151

7. C., 152

8. C., 152

9. B., 152

10. D., 154–155

11. D., 155

12. B., 157

13. D., 156

14. C., 156

15. B., 158

16. C., 159

17. D., 160

18. C., 161

19. C., 162

20. D., 163

Chapter 9

THE POLICE LEADER AS A COMMUNICATOR

SUMMARY

The individual who cannot communicate clearly and openly with his subordinates and superiors will not succeed as a police supervisor. It really is as simple as that.

Good communicators must understand others and be understood easily by them, both orally and in writing. They avoid such enemies to effective communication as distractions, prejudices, emotions, inappropriate language, and difficult attitudes. Instead, they communicate effectively with the sharing of information and ideas.

The intelligent police leader uses effective communication to help improve the efficiency and impact of the organization of which he is a part. He knows that an agency where ideas and information flow freely and accurately is an organization of contributing, trusting, and reasonably content employees. He knows, too, that by being a good communicator he can play a major role in making that positive scenario a reality.

QUESTIONS

1. It is almost impossible not to _____.

    a. Estimate
    b. Start rumors
    c. Prevaricate
    d. Communicate

2. The department's line-level leaders and the people they lead will be adversely affected if they feel they are being left out of the agency's _____.

    a. Grapevine
    b. Rumor mill
    c. Information flow
    d. Command Staff

3. _____ communication can create disorder and disunity in various parts of the organization.

    a. Poor
    b. Diverse
    c. Strong
    d. Interagency

4. Which is an element of good communication?

    a. Clear message
    b. Openness
    c. Two-way information flow
    d. All of the above

5. Which is also an element of good communications?

    a. Application of good listening/reading habits
    b. Calm approach
    c. Proper timing
    d. All of the above

6. Two-way _____ and respect are musts for effective communication.

    a. Hearing
    b. Awareness
    c. Trust
    d. Vision

7. A supervisor lacking in writing skills will seek to remedy the problem via _____.

    a. Practice
    b. Proofreading
    c. Both a and b
    d. Neither a nor b

8. Which is an enemy of good communication?

    a. Truth
    b. Grammar
    c. Distractions
    d. Spelling

9. Which is also an enemy of good communication?

    a. Prejudices
    b. Emotional involvement
    c. Inappropriate language
    d. All of the above

10. Good communication can and should mean _____ in the organization.

    a. More conflict
    b. Fewer misunderstandings
    c. Increased employee turnover
    d. Heightened turmoil

11. _____ communication is best in the person-to-person, one-on-one situation.

    a. Oral
    b. Written
    c. Unemotional
    d. Informal

12. The _____ comments of the supervisor are extremely vital in building the case for either praise or correction of an employee.

    a. Informal
    b. Oral
    c. Written
    d. Verbal

13. Effective communication can help improve the _____ and impact of the supervisor's organization.

    a. Efficiency
    b. Honesty
    c. Timeliness
    d. None of the above

14. Good communication requires the full _____ of the message sender and receiver.

    a. Coordination
    b. Attention
    c. Time
    d. Acceptance

15. The good communicator refrains from talking _____ to his audience.

    a. Loudly
    b. Forcefully
    c. Down
    d. Up

16. What kind of statements should be avoided in a leader's message to his employees?

    a. Disjointed
    b. Vague
    c. Ambiguous
    d. All of the above

17. Good _____ within the law enforcement organization allows subordinates and supervisors alike to feel better about themselves, their agency and each other.

    a. Attitudes
    b. Communication
    c. Vibes
    d. Karma

18. If the information in a message to be communicated is lengthy and/or complicated, it is generally best to _____.

    a. State it slowly
    b. Put it in writing
    c. Deliver it orally
    d. Deliver it in serial messages

19. If a message is to be in written form, the supervisor should keep the words, sentences, and paragraphs as _____ as possible for clarity and understanding.

    a. Simple
    b. Formal
    c. Informal
    d. Short

20. Whether the information being relayed is written or oral, its chances for reaching its intended listener/reader intact are reduced if it is surrounded by other happenings competing for _____.

    a. Time
    b. Emotional involvement
    c. Attention
    d. Processing

ANSWERS

1. D., 164

2. C., 165

3. A., 165

4. D., 166

5. D., 166–169

6. C., 173

7. C., 171

8. C., 175

9. D., 175

10. B., 180

11. A., 181

12. C., 182

13. A., 182

14. B., 183

15. C., 177

16. D., 167

17. B., 180

18. B., 166

19. D., 167

20. C., 175

Chapter 10

THE POLICE LEADER AS A COUNSELOR

SUMMARY

The police supervisor's role as a counselor and advisor is as delicate as it is vital to the employee, agency, and public. It is one that cannot be shirked except at great risk of neglecting supervisory responsibility.

The role is not one that can, in good faith, be left to another supervisor or the next person up the chain of command. It is only through accepting his sometimes uncomfortable but always necessary twin roles as problem solver and resource person that the leader-counselor can live up to the trust placed in him.

QUESTIONS

1. The concerned police supervisor will help both his employee and his organization through timely _____, when necessary.

    a. Promises
    b. Caution
    c. Intervention
    d. Warnings

2. Not all situations will be so obvious or so pressing as to require _____ intervention by the police supervisor.

    a. Postponed
    b. Indirect
    c. Direct
    d. Instant

3. Before the supervisor can help his people through counseling, he must first recognize the _____ of a developing problem.

    a. Length
    b. Size
    c. Existence
    d. Politics

4. What are the difficulties related to policing that may cause problems for employees that a supervisor may need to identify and address?

    a. Family problems caused by bizarre work hours with odd days off
    b. Less than outstanding working conditions
    c. Unanticipated scheduling changes
    d. All of the above

5. _____ is extremely influential in the world of the working cop.

    a. Peer pressure
    b. Use of force
    c. Use of minimal force
    d. Fear

6. Work problems, like illnesses, are attended by symptoms and often display _____.

   a. Mental illness
   b. Emotional trauma
   c. "Early warning signs"
   d. None of the above

7. Which of the following can be an indicator of a troubled employee?

   a. Alterations in appearance/grooming
   b. Abuse of sick leave
   c. Personality or mood changes
   d. All of the above

8. An employee who is signaling a problem by coming to work intoxicated requires _____.

   a. Immediate inquiry and action
   b. Sympathy
   c. Empathy
   d. Space

9. The effective supervisor-counselor pays attention to what an employee is _____ even if he thinks he has heard it all before.

   a. Showing
   b. Not really saying
   c. Saying
   d. None of the above

10. _____ is/are a must for the supervisor who intends to succeed as a counselor.

   a. Excellent listening skills
   b. Basic cynicism
   c. Good debating skills
   d. Mental health counselling skills

11. The process of dredging up all past grievances and alleged wrongs can be known as _____.

    a. Counselling
    b. Desensitization
    c. "Garbage bagging"
    d. "Emotional hoarding"

12. The counselor should allow plenty of _____ for a counselling discussion.

    a. Time
    b. Space
    c. Personal distance
    d. Emotional space

13. The police supervisor who has learned the art of empathetic counselling knows that he must guard the _____ of an employee experiencing personal problems.

    a. Reputation
    b. Back
    c. Privacy
    d. Career

14. If one is a supervisor, comparing his or her employee's problem to someone else's for the purpose of belittling the seriousness of the current difficulty is _____.

    a. Unwise
    b. An effective tactic
    c. Usually helpful
    d. Sometimes helpful

15. If a problem or difficulty detracts significantly from an employee's ability to do his job properly and safely, a _____ will be required.

    a. Suspension
    b. Temporary relief from duty
    c. Mental health evaluation
    d. Mental health hold

16. Now identified as a real disease, _____ does not lack for treatment programs to combat its effects.

    a. Cynicism
    b. Lack of trust
    c. Alcoholism
    d. Prejudice

17. With certain, limited exceptions such as illegal or improper conduct, the supervisor owes his employee _____ in the counseling relationship.

    a. Loyalty
    b. Caution
    c. Sympathy
    d. Confidentiality

18. The police supervisor's cardinal rule in his or her dealings with an employee of the opposite gender should be _____ in all things.

    a. Appearance
    b. Equality
    c. Preferential treatment
    d. Bias

19. Coaching and _____ go hand in hand.

    a. Chain of command
    b. Discipline
    c. Correction
    d. Mentoring

20. Sexual harassment represents a real and serious form of workplace _____ that cannot be allowed to exist in the law enforcement organization.

    a. Horseplay
    b. Conduct
    c. Joking
    d. Misconduct

ANSWERS

   1. C., 184

   2. D., 184

   3. C., 185

   4. D., 185–186

   5. A., 186

   6. C., 187

   7. D., 187–188

   8. A., 189

   9. C., 191

10. A., 191

11. C., 192

12. A., 192

13. C., 192

14. A., 192–193

15. B., 193

16. C., 195

17. D., 197

18. B., 199

19. D., 201

20. D., 202

Chapter 11

THE POLICE LEADER AS A MANAGER

SUMMARY

In serving in his manager's role, the police supervisor is not doing anything all that different from what he does daily as a front-line leader of law enforcement personnel. He is still directing, controlling, and coordinating activities in which people and things get the job done as well as possible. He is still giving direction and purpose to the efforts of others. He is assisting them where they face challenges or need the guidance of his experience. He is correcting or commending them for performances significantly below or above his expectations.

Some experts on management make rather much of the difference between front-line supervisors and their bosses, the mid-level managers. There are differences, true enough. The middle managers are generally seen as less involved in street-level aspects of policing and more concerned with the development of policy and procedure. However, the police organization that excludes its line supervisors from the exercise of their managerial skills in such areas as the creation of policy and procedure does so at its own peril. Law enforcement agencies that have allowed and encouraged contributions from their street-level supervisors have not infrequently been pleased with the pragmatic influences these people have brought to the final work product: service to the public.

Granted, the police supervisor's role should remain one which involves him or her in the front-line application and implementation of agency policy and procedure. This task, too, is a part of managerial responsibilities, and it generally must take precedence over any other duties. Just the same, to bar the supervisor from participating in the development of the guidelines that he will later implement will reduce the agency's effective-ness at the same time it hurts the morale and career development of a key member of the management team. Such waste must not be allowed to occur.

QUESTIONS

1. A manager in a police organization _____.

    a. Directs
    b. Controls
    c. Coordinates
    d. All of the above

2. The first-line supervisor should be involved in _____ affecting his unit's personnel.

    a. Investigations
    b. Conflicts
    c. Decisions
    d. None of the above

3. The police supervisor in his capacity as a manager serves as _____ for his subordinates.

    a. Role model
    b. Questioner
    c. Challenger
    d. Cover up

4. The effective manager utilizes _____ well when he relays it to those who will use it.

    a. Discipline
    b. Correction
    c. Information
    d. Punishment

5. The skilled and experienced police manager is a/an _____ for those beside him, above him, and below him in the chain of command.

    a. Peer
    b. Opponent
    c. Resource person
    d. Ally

6. Today's police officers are unwilling to be _____ rather than led.

   a. Assisted
   b. Directed
   c. Backed
   d. Driven

7. Serving in his manager's role in the area of community relations the supervisor should view himself as a/an _____ of his agency.

   a. Partner
   b. Protector
   c. Ambassador
   d. Supporter

8. As the police agency's representative in the community, the police supervisor will find that his manager's role includes the task of _____ of police actions and methods to a concerned public.

   a. Translator
   b. Defender
   c. Both a and b
   d. Neither a nor b

9. When the police supervisor-manager is handling a project or assignment for his boss, _____ must be known if he is to pace his work properly and not end up in a rush effort at the last moment.

   a. Potential costs
   b. Potential expenses
   c. Time constraints
   d. Potential threats

10. When the law enforcement supervisor-manager is putting together a written version of his work on a problem-oriented project, he should utilize a standard format including _____.

   a. Statement of the problem
   b. Recommended action or proposed solution
   c. Alternatives
   d. All of the above

11. Any lengthy, involved material inappropriate for the main body of a document prepared by the supervisor-manager should go into the _____.

    a. Contents
    b. Attachments or appendices
    c. Index
    d. Supplements

12. The sharp supervisor will avoid putting _____ in the written work that he submits.

    a. Technical terms
    b. Opinions
    c. Unnecessary words or padding
    d. All of the above

13. In the preparation of a final written accounting, the supervisor-manager's most useful tool(s) will be the _____.

    a. Support of his peers
    b. Rewrite and revision
    c. Support of his subordinates
    d. Dictionary

14. Confronted with a change in policy or procedure, the supervisor reviews it for completeness and _____ before he passes it on to others.

    a. Clarity
    b. Truth
    c. Technical details
    d. None of the above

15. The manager must accept _____ and be prepared to explain and support it to his subordinates.

    a. Error
    b. Change
    c. Criticism
    d. Uncertainty

16. A manager absolutely must be able to _____.

    a. Lie easily
    b. Prevaricate easily
    c. Know more than his people know
    d. Write clearly

17. The supervisor-manager _____ as he strives to obtain maximum effectiveness in all things.

    a. Rewards
    b. Corrects
    c. Counsels
    d. All of the above

18. The first-line supervisor should participate in decisions to grant _____ concerning his subordinates.

    a. Merit awards
    b. Pay bonuses
    c. Special recognition
    d. All of the above

19. The manager cannot be without _____ for his subordinates' earnest inquiries.

    a. Retorts
    b. Accurate replies
    c. Arguments
    d. Defenses

20. The police supervisor should remain mindful that since he does not like to receive _____ work from a subordinate, it is reasonable to assume that his boss does not like to receive it from him, either.

    a. Poor or incomplete
    b. Concise and direct
    c. Timely and accurate
    d. All of the above

ANSWERS

1. D., 204

2. C., 205

3. A., 205

4. C., 205

5. C., 207

6. D., 208

7. C., 208

8. C., 209

9. C., 209

10. D., 210

11. B., 211

12. C., 212

13. B., 217

14. A., 222

15. B., 223

16. D., 223

17. D., 203–204

18. D., 205

19. B., 208

20. A., 212

Chapter 12

THE POLICE LEADER AS A
COMPLAINT PROCESSOR

SUMMARY

The police leader must hear and address grievances, appeals, and complaints from a variety of sources. He must hear citizens' allegations of police misconduct and fairly investigate and follow up on them. He must receive employees' complaints against the law enforcement organization and its rules, regulations, policies, procedures, and staff actions and attempt to resolve them, too.

As the one in the middle, the supervisor must work to maintain his integrity and neutrality as he gives testimony in a disciplinary, labor, or appeal proceeding. It is all a part of his role as an impartial, patient, and responsive complaint processor for other peoples' grievances. It is a role vital in the well-being of the citizens, the employees, and the management of the agency he serves.

QUESTIONS

1. In some cases in which he has received a complaint or grievance the law enforcement supervisor's job will be that of a/an _____.

   a. Obstacle
   b. Careful reporter
   c. Union steward
   d. All of the above

2. The manner in which the supervisor _____ can have much to do with the future attitude and well-being of the complainant, the concerned employees, and the police organization as a whole.

   a. Reacts to the complaint
   b. Pursues a fair and thorough inquiry
   c. Arrives at concrete results
   d. All of the above

3. Police agencies receive and process complaints against their personnel, procedures, and policies for several good reasons, including _____.

   a. To protect the public from actual police misconduct
   b. To protect police employees from unjust allegations
   c. To protect the credibility and integrity of the police agency
   d. All of the above

4. What is yet another legitimate reason why police agencies receive and process complaints against their personnel, procedures, and policies?

   a. To shield the city manager from criticism
   b. To shield the mayor from political fallout
   c. To detect and correct improper or inadequate operating procedures or policies
   d. None of the above

5. Good employee _____ and training can do much to prevent many of the problems and abuses connected with police corruption, incompetency, or abuse of authority.

   a. Selection
   b. Comprehension
   c. Understanding
   d. All of the above

6. The well-organized law enforcement agency will allow its first-line supervisors a good deal of _____ of handling minor complaints and inquiries regarding policy, procedure or officer conduct.

   a. Self-discipline
   b. Discretion
   c. Both a and b
   d. Neither a nor b

7. _____ is an example of an inquiry or complaint situation that can and should be handled by a first-line supervisor.

   a. General questions on departmental policies
   b. Inquiries regarding use of force guidelines
   c. Inquiries on handcuff use
   d. All of the above

8. _____ is an example of the kind of complaint that would demand a deeper look at the facts as opposed to a cursory handling of the situation by a first-line supervisor.

   a. Complaints of false arrest
   b. Complaints of police excessive force
   c. Complaints of criminal acts by police employees
   d. All of the above

9. More serious allegations of misconduct by police employees will require more _____ investigations.

   a. Truthful
   b. Competent
   c. In-depth
   d. Accurate

10. If what the supervisor knows about an incident or allegation includes even the slightest hint that criminal conduct has occurred,
he is obligated to give the employee what has come to be termed
the _____.

    a. *Mapp v. Ohio* advisement
    b. *Loudermill* advisement
    c. *Terry* advisement
    d. *Garrity* advisement

11. The supervisor should electronically _____ a lengthy or complex
interview, in addition to taking detailed notes.

    a. Record
    b. Text
    c. E-mail
    d. Redact

12. Following an allegation of police employee misconduct, the _____
must receive notification of the results of the investigation.

    a. Supervisor
    b. Suspect
    c. Complainant
    d. Elected officials

13. _____ heads the list of causes for internal squabbling in many
police agencies.

    a. Use of force
    b. "Lack of communication"
    c. Use of excessive force
    d. None of the above

14. Communications-conscious police supervisors encourage the officers under them to engage in _____ with police personnel else-
where, within and without their department.

    a. Debate
    b. Critical debate
    c. Free exchange of information
    d. Honest debate

15. The wise supervisor will keep his ears open for indications of real or imagined internal problems involving his team or work unit and then _____.

    a. Act to ascertain the validity of the information
    b. Identify the difficulty
    c. Take action to resolve the issue
    d. All of the above

16. The police supervisor engaged at any stage of the grievance proceeding must remain mindful of his _____ to employees and management.

    a. Equal obligations
    b. Truth
    c. Both a and b
    d. Neither a nor b

17. Which is a typical concern of the police labor organization?

    a. Increased job security
    b. No retribution for union activities
    c. Improved salary and benefits
    d. All of the above

18. Which is a tactic sometimes employed by a law enforcement labor organization to get a point across?

    a. Enforcement speedup
    b. Enforcement slowdown
    c. "Blue flu"
    d. All of the above

19. During a police management-police labor dispute, the supervisor does not tolerate _____ and initiates appropriate investigative and corrective measures.

    a. Improper police behavior
    b. Insubordination
    c. Neglect of duty
    d. All of the above

20. The supervisor has a/an _____ role to play in receiving and in-vestigating citizen and employee complaints.

    a. Minor
    b. Occasional
    c. Key
    d. None of the above

ANSWERS

1. B., 224

2. D., 225

3. D., 225

4. C., 225

5. A., 225–226

6. B., 226

7. D., 229

8. D., 229

9. C., 229

10. D., 231

11. A., 232

12. C., 238

13. B., 239

14. C., 240

15. D., 240

16. A., 242

17. D., 243

18. D., 244–245

19. D., 246

20. C., 247

Chapter 13

SOME SPECIAL PROBLEMS

SUMMARY

With luck, the average police supervisor may never have to work for a rotten boss or confront a serious incidence of police malpractice during a whole career of leadership. With more and more people of high moral fiber and good common sense entering the police profession, the possibility of never encountering such malignancies increases steadily.

Nonetheless, the supervisor who would be thoroughly skilled in his calling and truly ready to handle any special problem that might come along readies himself for these, too. It is just another set of challenges to be capably addressed by the common sense supervisor.

QUESTIONS

1. It has been said that the first-line supervisor is something of a _____.

   a. Hybrid creation
   b. Question mark
   c. Conflicted individual
   d. All of the above

2. The first-line supervisor is often not considered a/an _____ part of either the street officers or upper management.

   a. Credible
   b. Intimate
   c. Believable
   d. Loyal

3. Many if not most supervisors can at least _____ a dreamed-about career change.

   a. Research
   b. Try
   c. Implement
   d. None of the above

4. The intelligent police supervisor will engage in some realistic _____ of who he is, where he is, and where he would like to be some day.

   a. Arguments
   b. Daydreaming
   c. Assessments
   d. Debates

5. The dissatisfied but intelligent supervisor will avoid making momentous decisions, career-related or otherwise, during moments of _____.

   a. Personal depression or unhappiness
   b. Victory and happiness
   c. Great joy
   d. Minor change

6. The old saying of _____ could prove invaluable to the marginally dissatisfied supervisor.

   a. "Do unto others"
   b. "Size matters"
   c. "Take a walk in my shoes"
   d. "Look before you leap"

7. The intelligent supervisor will bring _____ and common sense to his career planning deliberations.

   a. Subjectivity
   b. Diversity
   c. Objectivity
   d. None of the above

8. The police organization has its _____ and informal codes of conduct for its supervisors.

   a. Unethical rules
   b. Unwritten rules
   c. Untested rules
   d. All of the above

9. Along with field survival, the wise police supervisor will pay heed to the rules of _____ survival.

   a. Managerial
   b. Leadership
   c. Labor
   d. Organizational

10. An organizational survivor knows better than to _____ the decisions and actions of his peers.

    a. Back
    b. Second-guess
    c. Support
    d. Learn from

11. The wise supervisor knows that a/an _____ boss is most often a reasonably content leader, and he avoids keeping important facts from him.

    a. Informed
    b. Ill-advised
    c. Ill-informed
    d. Delusional

12. For the effective law enforcement supervisor, _____ not constant controversy, is the key to getting things done.

    a. Discussion
    b. Debate
    c. Cooperation
    d. Congeniality

13. People in general and police officers in particular are diligent in their efforts at _____.

    a. Rumor-mongering
    b. Arguing
    c. Prevaricating
    d. Exaggerating

14. The _____ supervisor devotes much of his energy to promoting internal feuds, holding grudges, and provoking disputes.

    a. Short-sighted
    b. Egotistical
    c. Probably ineffective
    d. All of the above

15. The wise and effective supervisor can protect others at the same time he helps himself by discouraging a climate in which _____ can take place by rumor-mongering.

    a. Career advancement
    b. Leadership
    c. Character assassination
    d. All of the above

16. _____ in the law enforcement organization is as destructive to employee morale as it is to the quality of service provided to the public.

    a. Use of force
    b. Internal strife
    c. Open discussion
    d. Promotion

17. Political corruption and misconduct _____ today.

    a. Still exist
    b. Do not exist
    c. Are accepted
    d. Should be tolerated within reason

18. Fair treatment and reasonable accommodations for persons with handicaps are the just expectations of the _____.

    a. *Brady* decision
    b. *Garrity* decision
    c. Americans with Disabilities Act (ADA)
    d. Fair Labor Standards Act (FLSA)

19. Confronting a boss problem honestly and tactfully is _____ the best way of addressing it.

    a. Never
    b. Occasionally
    c. Oftentimes
    d. Seldom

20. Sexual and racial harassment are a/an _____ concern for the police leader today.

    a. Rare
    b. Major
    c. Lesser
    d. Minor

ANSWERS

1. A., 249

2. B., 249

3. A., 251

4. C., 252

5. A., 252

6. D., 251

7. C., 252

8. B., 253

9. D., 252

10. B., 253

11. A., 254

12. C., 255

13. A., 255

14. D., 255

15. C., 256

16. B., 257

17. A., 260

18. C., 263

19. C., 267–268

20. B., 263

Chapter 14

THE POLICE LEADER'S ROLE
IN COMMUNITY POLICING

SUMMARY

Supervision in a police agency practicing true community policing requires a partial break with the traditional style of law enforcement supervision. But supervision is not lacking. It is simply somewhat different in its approach and application. The effective community policing supervisor still guides, assists, and evaluates his people and their work. But he also grants them additional independence, flexibility, and authority to identify problems and secure the community's active assistance in solving them. In the final analysis, he emphasizes effectiveness over numbers; obvious results over older ways.

Community policing does not weaken supervision. It merely redirects some of its focus.

QUESTIONS

1. Community-oriented policing or simply community policing is _____ for American law enforcement in the early twenty-first century.

   a. The "Next Big Thing"
   b. The preferred way of doing business
   c. A passing fad
   d. The latest fad

2. When properly done, community-oriented policing is _____.

   a. "Police social work"
   b. Not "police social work"
   c. Sometimes correctly referred to as "police social work"
   d. Counselling and referrals

3. Individual officers working in a community policing structure seek to be _____ as opposed to reactive in their approach to their duties.

   a. Restrained
   b. Responsive
   c. Proactive
   d. Laid back

4. Community policing requires _____ on the part of the police professional.

   a. Problem solution
   b. Problem referral
   c. Problem deferral
   d. Problem shifting

5. Community policing in its true form exists only where the _____ or some element of it in addition to the police participate(s) in problem identification, analysis, and solution.

   a. Top elected official
   b. Department leadership
   c. Command Staff
   d. Community

6. Community policing is a philosophy or _____ for an entire law enforcement operation or organization.

   a. Discipline
   b. Mantra
   c. Mindset
   d. Dogma

7. The idea of community policing is to involve police officers with _____ living, working, or playing in a given area to identify problems and mutually develop solutions for them.

   a. Critics
   b. Minorities
   c. Citizens
   d. None of the above

8. Even in locales where the concept of community-oriented policing is fully embraced, police will always have to be _____ at times, as well.

   a. Offensive
   b. Reactive
   c. Cautionary
   d. Punitive

9. Community policing is not intended to be _____.

   a. A public relations trick
   b. Warm and fuzzy
   c. Soft on criminals
   d. All of the above

10. Community policing is a/an _____ operation.

    a. Specialized unit
    b. Veteran officer
    c. All hands
    d. Uniformed

11. Advocates for community policing note that it is the _____ who most often determine(s) if community-oriented policing will succeed.

    a. First-line officers
    b. First-line supervisors
    c. Agency head
    d. Command Staff

12. Indifference or hostility from the _____ will make it hard for community policing to work, even if the police brass supports it.

    a. Mid-managers
    b. News media
    c. Police critics
    d. Supervisory corps

13. Encouraging officers to innovate and _____ to old problems is what community policing is about.

    a. Turn their backs
    b. Show less attention
    c. Develop new responses
    d. None of the above

14. Community policing will force the traditional system supervisor to make some changes in what he _____ as well as in what he prizes in a subordinate.

    a. Monitors
    b. Disciplines
    c. Corrects
    d. Punishes

15. Community policing _____ employees' accountability to their supervisor.

    a. Reduces
    b. Does not reduce
    c. Changes radically
    d. Doubles

16. Good community policing leaders _____ among their subordinates.

    a. Build trust
    b. Build a positive attitude
    c. Both a and b
    d. Neither a nor b

17. _____ by the first-line supervisor is necessary if the community-oriented approach to solving problems is going to work well.

    a. Close supervision
    b. Loose supervision
    c. Disinterest
    d. Continuing interest

18. In community policing, supervisors provide their officers with a reasonable degree of earned independence and allow them to "fail" _____ by learning from the experience without major repercussions.

    a. Successfully
    b. Totally
    c. Partially
    d. Organizationally

19. Supervision in a police agency practicing true community policing requires a _____ break with the traditional style of law enforcement supervision.

    a. Complete
    b. Total
    c. Partial
    d. None of the above

20. The effective community policing supervisor grants his employees additional _____ to identify problems and secure the community's active assistance in solving them.

    a. Independence
    b. Flexibility
    c. Authority
    d. All of the above

ANSWERS

1. B., 270

2. B., 271

3. C., 271

4. A., 271

5. D., 271

6. C., 270

7. C., 271

8. B., 272

9. D., 273

10. C., 273

11. B., 274

12. D., 274

13. C., 275

14. A., 275

15. B., 276

16. C., 277

17. D., 277

18. A., 278

19. C., 278

20. D., 278

Chapter 15

THE POLICE LEADER'S ROLE
IN OFFICER SURVIVAL

SUMMARY

In no aspect of his important job are the police supervisor's attitudes and actions more vital to his subordinates' welfare than in the area of officer safety. The effective supervisor helps his officers survive on the street by constantly assessing their safety-related practices and providing training and counseling where needed. He inspects his troops' safety equipment and ensures that they know how to use it well. He intervenes and, where necessary, corrects when their officer safety practices are unacceptable. He helps with their emotional survival and explains their safety practices to others when questions arise. Most important of all, he serves as an excellent role model for good safety awareness and survival practices.

QUESTIONS

1. The officer safety errors that have resulted in police casualties have changed _____ over the years.

   a. Greatly
   b. In scope
   c. Little
   d. Much

2. A major killer of police officers is _____.

   a. Making false assumptions
   b. Poor positioning or approach
   c. General carelessness and apathy
   d. All of the above

3. An additional, major fatal error sometimes committed by police officers is _____.

   a. Failure to watch a subject's hands
   b. Poor searches of subjects
   c. Failure to wear body armor
   d. All of the above

4. For peace officers, a step for staying alive includes _____.

   a. Use greater force than necessary
   b. Do not underestimate your adversary
   c. Get in close quickly
   d. All of the above

5. An additional step for staying alive is _____.

   a. Make the best use of available cover
   b. Follow proper handcuffing and searching procedures
   c. Use backup help wisely
   d. All of the above

6. Which of the following is not valid advice for staying alive on the street?

   a. Stay in shape, both mentally and physically
   b. Watch your subject's eyes, not his hands
   c. Practice good weapon retention tactics
   d. All of the above

7. In order to learn from his experiences, the wise law enforcement officer will _____ his officer safety practices.

   a. Redouble
   b. Reinforce
   c. Critique
   d. All of the above

8. It is the primary supervisor's job to _____ proper safety and survival behavior for his or her subordinates.

   a. Model
   b. Criticize
   c. Minimize
   d. None of the above

9. The alert police supervisor need not concern himself with the safety and survival training needs of the _____ employee.

   a. Veteran
   b. Rookie
   c. Underperforming
   d. None of the above

10. The police supervisor's safety training job is a/an _____ one.

    a. Unpopular
    b. Unending
    c. Thankless
    d. Unrewarded

11. The supervisor's safety counselling task may become somewhat harder when it comes to the _____ employee who feels he or she has seen it all, done it all, and knows it all.

    a. Generation X
    b. Baby Boomer
    c. Veteran
    d. Generation Y

12. Closely related to the supervisor's responsibility to train for safety is his obligation to _____ for it.

    a. Punish
    b. Warn
    c. Correct
    d. Inspect

13. The law enforcement supervisor must carefully observe and assess real-world tactics including _____.

    a. Approach
    b. Positioning
    c. Use of cover
    d. All of the above

14. The safety-savvy police supervisor teaches officer survival _____.

    a. In the classroom
    b. At every opportunity
    c. To his rookie officers
    d. If permitted by union contract

15. The supervisor _____ promptly when he detects unsafe practices by his subordinates.

    a. Punishes
    b. Disciplines
    c. Intervenes
    d. Documents

16. The effective police supervisor serves as an excellent _____ for officer safety practices.

    a. Role model
    b. Disciplinarian
    c. Manager
    d. Representative

17. If a "cowboy" cop cannot be brought to mend his dangerously unsafe ways and work within the expectations of the law enforcement organization, for everyone's good he must be _____.

    a. Placed in a special assignment
    b. Promoted off of the street
    c. Separated from the police service
    d. Given a desk job

18. Sometimes the police supervisor has an excellent opportunity to _____ the public about the dangers and difficulties of the cop's job.

    a. Caution
    b. Educate
    c. Propagandize
    d. Warn

19. The survival-conscious police supervisor develops a work team of _____ officers around him.

    a. Safety-smart
    b. Veteran
    c. Suspicious
    d. Hardened

20. A good police supervisor watches out for his employees' _____ survival, too.

    a. Supervisory
    b. Union
    c. Emotional
    d. Marital

ANSWERS

1. C., 280

2. D., 280–281

3. D., 281

4. B., 281

5. D., 281

6. B., 281

7. C., 282

8. A., 282

9. D., 283

10. B., 283

11. C., 283

12. D., 283

13. D., 284

14. B., 289

15. C., 289

16. A., 289

17. C., 286

18. B., 287

19. A., 288

20. C., 289

Chapter 16

THE POLICE LEADER AS
AGENCY SPOKESPERSON

SUMMARY

The public gets most of its information about law enforcement officers and law enforcement operations from internet news, television, motion pictures, radio, and the print media. Clearly it is in the best interest of the supervisor, his employer, and the policing profession that all information reaching the public is accurate and, whenever possible, presents law enforcement and its people in a positive light. That does not obligate the ethical law enforcement leader to lick anyone's boots or otherwise "kiss up" to the press. It does mean that the police supervisor who deals competently, honestly, and fairly with the media on the scene of a crime or other interest-generating incident makes it more likely that his agency will be fairly-treated when the news hits the airwaves or the morning's headlines.

The intelligent leader prepares carefully for his "fifteen seconds" in the media spotlight. He gets his facts straight, plans, and practices what he wants to say ahead of time and then says it—clearly, concisely, and briefly. He follows his department's rules for what he can and cannot release, but everything he does say is the truth. He aids the media's representatives in every way that he legitimately can, but he does not permit them to run rampant or otherwise interfere with a crime scene or police operation.

Any police supervisor can contribute to good news media relations for his department when he is on the spot and on the news. All it takes is the application of attention to detail, good judgment, common sense, and an absolute devotion to telling the truth. Chances are each of those key tools is already in the toolbox of the competent law enforcement leader.

QUESTIONS

1. What should the police supervisor do when preparing to respond to questions from the news media?

   a. Get the facts
   b. Double check the facts for accuracy
   c. Organize the facts for presentation
   d. All of the above

2. In releasing information to the press, the supervisor turned spokesperson will avoid _____.

   a. Guessing
   b. Speculating
   c. Passing along anything he does not know for certain to be true
   d. All of the above

3. In law enforcement's relationship with the press, it is vital that police not be the source for _____.

   a. Incorrect information
   b. On-scene statements
   c. Violent descriptions
   d. All of the above

4. For all practical purposes, once information from law enforcement is in the hands of the press it _____ recalled.

   a. Can be
   b. Cannot be
   c. Generally can be
   d. Sometimes can be

5. It is _____ acceptable for a law enforcement supervisor to ask a newsperson what he or she plans to ask in an upcoming interview.

   a. Never
   b. Perfectly
   c. Sometimes
   d. Seldom

6. Before the police leader steps in front of the press to make a statement or answer questions, he or she should make an effort to _____ what is to be said.

   a. Exaggerate
   b. Fabricate
   c. Practice
   d. None of the above

7. One reliable way in which a police leader can determine the facts he needs to assemble to do a media interview is to _____.

   a. Ask his supervisor
   b. Place himself in the reporter's shoes
   c. Ask the Public Information Officer
   d. None of the above

8. Appropriate guidelines governing the release of information to the news media include(s) _____.

   a. Do furnish an overview of the crime or incident
   b. Do identify yourself and provide a telephone number and e-mail address where you can be reached, if necessary
   c. Do provide the name of a follow-up contact person
   d. All of the above

9. Appropriate guidelines governing the nonrelease of information to the news media include(s) _____.

   a. Don't comment on evidence, such as a confession
   b. Don't release the names of deceased persons until the next of kin have been notified
   c. Don't give out information that may become an investigative key
   d. All of the above

10. _____ is everything to a police leader, in press matters as well as in everything else he says or does.

    a. Proven toughness
    b. Glibness
    c. Credibility
    d. None of the above

11. According to one highly-acclaimed journalist, credibility in an interviewee comes from _____.

    a. Openness
    b. Willingness to take questions
    c. Understanding that most reporters are just trying to do the job they are paid to do
    d. All of the above

12. It is important that the police supervisor remains _____ during his encounter with a reporter or photojournalist and respond with patience and courtesy.

    a. Suspicious
    b. Calm and in control
    c. On the offensive
    d. On the defensive

13. Before doing a television news interview, the supervisor should _____.

    a. Assemble the needed facts
    b. Double-check the facts for accuracy
    c. Practice what he/she plans to say
    d. All of the above

14. During an on-camera television interview, the supervisor-spokesperson should look at _____.

    a. The camera
    b. The camera lens
    c. The interviewer
    d. The microphone

15. The supervisor-spokesperson should treat all cameras or microphones in his presence as _____ at all times.

    a. "Live"
    b. "Deadly"
    c. "An opportunity"
    d. "Dead"

16. Which is a reasonable restriction to be placed by law enforcement on news-gathering activities by the media?

   a. The media cannot be allowed to destroy evidence or otherwise contaminate a crime scene
   b. The media cannot be allowed to obstruct or interfere with police operations on-scene
   c. Members of the media must not be allowed or assisted to break the law
   d. All of the above

17. A good rule of thumb for the police leader enforcing media restrictions on-scene is this common sense piece of advice: _____.

   a. Look before you leap
   b. Walk before you run
   c. Have a good reason for what you do
   d. All of the above

18. Intentionally providing false information to the media is _____.

   a. Sometimes necessary
   b. Unethical
   c. Unofficial
   d. Off the books

19. _____ is good advice for the law enforcement supervisor tasked with preparing a news release.

   a. Include the "5 Ws and an H"
   b. It must be right
   c. Keep it short
   d. All of the above

20. _____ represents more good advice for the law enforcement supervisor involved in writing a news release.

   a. Do not overuse it
   b. Avoid giving opinions in it
   c. Get any required approvals
   d. All of the above

ANSWERS

1. D., 291

2. D., 292

3. A., 292

4. B., 293

5. B., 293

6. C., 293

7. B., 292

8. D., 294

9. D., 294

10. C., 294–295

11. D., 295

12. B., 295

13. D., 296

14. C., 297

15. A., 297

16. D., 298

17. C., 298

18. B., 305

19. D., 301–302

20. D., 302

Chapter 17

THE POLICE LEADER'S ROLE IN EXCEPTIONAL CUSTOMER SERVICE

SUMMARY

Good customer service contains heaping measures of basic courtesy and plain common sense. It really is common in good organizations, law enforcement organizations included. It is not a mysterious or unattainable commodity. It the final analysis, good customer service amounts to little more than a version of the Golden Rule: TREAT OTHERS AS YOU WOULD LIKE TO BE TREATED YOURSELF.

The police leader who demands exceptional customer service from his subordinates role models it himself in all of his contacts with his organization's internal as well as external customers. He rewards employees displaying it and he corrects and trains them when he finds it lacking. Information furnished in this chapter can be provided to his employees by the leader interested in improving the customer service that they provide. It is in this way that he helps assure that law enforcement gets better and his citizen-customers get served in the manner they deserve.

That is, after all, what truly exceptional customer service is about.

QUESTIONS

1. Too many citizens view law enforcement people as _____.

   a. Public servants
   b. Heroes
   c. Bureaucrats
   d. Public safety specialists

2. Experience has demonstrated that the police employee who utilizes some basic customer service skills in his interactions with people will find those same people _____.

   a. Generally resistant
   b. Uncooperative
   c. Easier to handle
   d. Obstructive

3. Which is a key guideline employed by entities enjoying a reputation for great customer service?

   a. Customers are very important to us
   b. Customers are the reason we have a job
   c. Customers are individuals with names and feelings
   d. All of the above

4. Most people are, at worst, _____ in their reaction to police authority.

   a. Welcoming
   b. Neutral
   c. Hostile
   d. None of the above

5. The average citizen expects what in his interaction with a police customer service provider?

   a. Reliability
   b. Responsiveness
   c. Reassurance
   d. All of the above

6. What is a phrase from a customer service provider that may help furnish reassurance to a citizen-customer?

   a. "The worst is over."
   b. "It's going to be alright."
   c. Both a and b
   d. Neither a nor b

7. What is an additional "something" the average citizen expects from a customer service provider?

   a. Empathy
   b. Results
   c. Both a and b
   d. Neither a nor b

8. What does a citizen-customer NOT want to hear from a service provider?

   a. "You should have called earlier."
   b. "That's impossible."
   c. "That's department policy."
   d. All of the above

9. What else does a citizen-customer NOT want to hear from a service provider?

   a. "I can't help you."
   b. "I understand what you are going through."
   c. "I am sorry this has happened to you."
   d. All of the above

10. On a national scale, frequently heard customer complaints include _____.

    a. Rudeness; discourtesy
    b. Attitude of indifference
    c. "Nobody listened to me."
    d. All of the above

11. The customer service failures that truly upset customers are _____ from one part of the nation to the next.

   a. Varied
   b. Fairly consistent
   c. Very different
   d. Inconsistent

12. The steps to providing good customer service include an honest expression of _____ and a sincere willingness to help on the part of the service provider.

   a. Professionalism
   b. Doubt
   c. Concern
   d. Denial

13. A basic "trick of the trade" for increasing customer satisfaction is _____.

   a. Be a very good listener
   b. Allow the customer to save face, if possible
   c. Treat people as individuals and use their name
   d. All of the above

14. Another basic "trick of the trade" for increasing customer satisfaction is _____.

   a. Build trust
   b. Avoid direct eye contact
   c. Speak loudly
   d. All of the above

15. Good police communicators _____.

   a. Make good eye contact with the customer
   b. Display an open posture
   c. Avoid cop talk or police slang
   d. All of the above

16. Exceptional customer service flows from employees who _____.

    a. Avoid stating the unpleasant
    b. Display a "no tolerance" posture
    c. Display excellent communication skills
    d. Display a "no nonsense" demeanor

17. Good police communicators stress what they _____ do to help the citizen-customer.

    a. Cannot
    b. Can
    c. Might
    d. Should

18. In attempting to defuse an unhappy customer, it may be helpful to _____.

    a. Stress the ultimate authority of the law
    b. Deny accountability
    c. Try to reach agreement on SOMETHING
    d. Defer accountability

19. It is _____ to confront inaccurate statements made by an angry or upset complainant.

    a. Acceptable
    b. Never acceptable
    c. A bad idea
    d. A questionable tactic

20. _____, or a lack thereof, are often a very good indicator of the overall health of customer service in a business or government agency.

    a. Telephone manners
    b. Good salary and benefits
    c. Poor salary and benefits
    d. Strong policies and procedures

ANSWERS

1. C., 306

2. C., 307

3. D., 307

4. B., 308

5. D., 308

6. C., 308

7. C., 308

8. D., 308–309

9. A., 309

10. D., 309

11. B., 309

12. C., 310

13. D., 310

14. A., 311

15. D., 311

16. C., 311

17. B., 311–312

18. C., 313

19. A., 313

20. A., 314

Chapter 18

WORKING FOR SOMEONE

SUMMARY

Everyone has a boss. Or several of them. The law enforcement leader is going to work under the supervision of someone. That someone can help to make or break a career. The smart law enforcement supervisor will do everything appropriate and reasonable to assure that the boss-subordinate relationship is a positive one. In the process, the supervised is likely to learn some important things to do (and not do) that will boost his or her career while building a positive supervisor-supervised relationship.

While there may be a number of reasons why a given supervisor fails to reach his or her full potential, somewhere near the top of the list is failure to connect effectively with the boss. That reality holds true whether the boss is a pleasure to work with or something else entirely. An atmosphere of mutual trust and respect must exist for the working relationship to be a good one. Adhering to a set of cardinal rules for a favorable supervisor-supervised relationship will help you guarantee that this kind of atmosphere prevails.

QUESTIONS

1. Bosses want to be told _____.

   a. The truth
   b. What they want to hear
   c. As little as possible
   d. None of the above

2. Bosses expect and appreciate _____ during trying times.

   a. Procrastination
   b. Privacy
   c. Support
   d. All the above

3. Loyalty to the boss does not mean _____ loyalty.

   a. Sincere
   b. Blind
   c. Honest
   d. Total

4. The loyal subordinate does not _____ his boss's decisions.

   a. Low
   b. Mid-range
   c. Out of the box
   d. Criticize

5. The subordinate should provide his or her boss with _____ professional advice and knowledge when needed.

   a. Semi-confidential
   b. Competent
   c. Conditional
   d. Tentative

6. The subordinate should furnish his or her boss with information and advice in a manner that is unlikely to leave him feeling _____.

   a. Smarter
   b. Informed
   c. Ridiculed
   d. Competent

7. Most bosses appreciate subordinates who _____ for extra assignments.

   a. Yearn
   b. Prevaricate
   c. Beg
   d. Volunteer

8. Your boss will not appreciate being _____ or embarrassed.

   a. Denied
   b. Humored
   c. Surprised
   d. Shocked

9. Not unlike you, your boss would prefer to be _____ by you as opposed to the opposite.

   a. Surprised
   b. Shocked
   c. Displeased
   d. Over-informed

10. An unwise supervisor publicly _____ his or her boss for unpopular decisions.

   a. Prevaricates
   b. Praises
   c. Blames
   d. Questions

11. As a law enforcement leader, you should never display fear or _____ in front of your supervisor.

    a. Self-confidence
    b. Self-doubt
    c. Decisiveness
    d. Courage

12. Your boss will expect that you as a competent supervisor will not _____ to your subordinates.

    a. Pander
    b. Display disappointment
    c. Display pride
    d. Display chagrin

13. It is very likely that your boss does not want you to participate in organizational _____.

    a. Support
    b. Teamwork
    c. Staffing
    d. Intrigue

14. Your meeting with a difficult boss should not commence with your making _____.

    a. Statements
    b. Pleasantries
    c. Trouble
    d. Accusations

15. Complaining to your boss's boss about him or her should be considered your _____ option.

    a. First
    b. Best
    c. Immediate
    d. Nuclear

16. Confronting a difficult boss _____ is often the best way of addressing the situation.

    a. Quickly and emotionally
    b. Reluctantly and emotionally
    c. Emotionally and stridently
    d. Honestly but tactfully

17. The career-wise supervisor will make it clear to his or her boss that he or she wants to learn the boss's _____.

    a. Feelings
    b. Tricks
    c. Biases
    d. Job

18. To further your own career, you will want a good boss to _____ you.

    a. Mentor
    b. Coach
    c. Educate
    d. All the above

19. Excellent _____ will have to exist between you and your boss if you are to excel as a leader in your law enforcement organization.

    a. Communication
    b. Mutual trust
    c. Mutual respect
    d. All of the above

20. As an effective leader, you should be keenly aware of the _____ of your supervisor.

    a. History
    b. Background
    c. Expectations
    d. Future

ANSWERS

1. A., 318

2. C., 318

3. B., 318

4. D., 318-319

5. B., 319

6. C., 319

7. D., 319

8. C., 320

9. D., 320

10. C., 320-321

11. B., 321

12. A., 321

13. D., 322

14. D., 324

15. D., 325

16. D., 325

17. D., 327

18. D., 327

19. D., 327-328

20. C., 328

Chapter 19

WHERE DO I GO FROM HERE?

SUMMARY

The law enforcement supervisor's career planning begins today and should continue throughout a long work life. Periodic reassessment and redirection may be required, but planning must continue all the same. Challenges and even opposition are likely to be encountered en route, but the effective supervisor is a stranger to neither. He should not underestimate his own abilities in seeking advancement. By making contacts, gathering information, and seeking advice from reliable sources he will close the gap between himself and his next career advancement post. By avoiding personal and career mistakes, he will continue to prepare himself for the next step on the career ladder.

The upward-climbing supervisor will hone his communication and leadership skills throughout a career. He will volunteer for greater responsibilities and prepare himself to assume his boss's job one day. He will not underestimate the possibilities or his own abilities. For many leaders, winning the position of head of the organization is not beyond reach.

It all starts with planning "Where Do I Go From Here?"

QUESTIONS

1. All law enforcement agencies need plenty of competent _____.

   a. Internal critics
   b. First-line leaders
   c. Outside critics
   d. Monday morning quarterbacks

2. The career-planning supervisor will carefully examine the possibilities for _____ in his current agency.

   a. Political alliances
   b. Intrigue
   c. Advancement
   d. Internal dissent

3. Leadership career planning should start with _____.

   a. An open and honest discussion at home
   b. A meeting with the chief
   c. A formal meeting with one's supervisor
   d. An open discussion with one's peers at work

4. The career planner should keep his goals _____.

   a. Low
   b. Mid-range
   c. Out of the box
   d. Realistic

5. In planning his career, the police supervisor needs to have some idea of the _____ he is talking about.

   a. Politics
   b. Organizational infighting
   c. Timeframe
   d. Money

6. Changing one's goals along the career path is _____.

    a. A dubious practice
    b. Acceptable
    c. A practice to be discouraged
    d. Seldom a good idea

7. The sharp supervisor interested in career advancement always will remain _____ enough to handle the good and bad surprises of the job.

    a. Flexible
    b. Focused
    c. Cynical
    d. None of the above

8. The supervisor intent on planning intelligently for the future will invest some time in _____ the possibilities.

    a. Imagining
    b. Researching
    c. Planning
    d. Dreaming

9. The police supervisor intent upon climbing the career advancement ladder must avoid a number of _____.

    a. Career killers
    b. Disciplinary actions
    c. Reassignments
    d. Specialized assignments

10. The supervisor with a knack for organizational survival will not ally himself with a mentor seen as a/an _____ in the organization.

    a. Production leader
    b. Informal leader
    c. "Problem"
    d. Formal leader

11. Bosses often watch how a subordinate handles _____.

   a. Physical disabilities
   b. Adversity
   c. Rank
   d. Diversity

12. The supervisor with his sights set on career advancement will be aware of the _____ of the position he is seeking.

   a. Personality-shifting requirements
   b. Monetary requirements
   c. Educational requirements
   d. None of the above

13. It is absolutely necessary that the supervisor interested in career advancement _____.

   a. Let his peers know of his interest
   b. Let his boss know of his interest
   c. Let his subordinates know of his interest
   d. Tell himself of his interest

14. Career planning for today's law enforcement leader should include planning for _____.

   a. Political repercussions
   b. Tomorrow
   c. Yesterday
   d. Life beyond the badge

15. A good _____ can provide an interested, respectful supervisor with the political lay of the land of the organization to which they both belong.

   a. Colleague
   b. Mentor
   c. Peer
   d. Shop steward

16. _____ are good people to know for the individual wishing to lead law enforcement agency one day.

    a. Political appointees
    b. Elected officials
    c. Retired officers
    d. Executive search consultants

17. The law enforcement supervisor seeking to advance his career needs to be _____.

    a. Aggressive without being obnoxious
    b. Persistent without becoming a pest
    c. Both a and b
    d. Neither a nor b

18. What is a useful guideline for the police supervisor preparing a resume?

    a. Never use a generic resume
    b. Proof, proof, and proof again to detect errors
    c. Tell the truth and do not exaggerate accomplishments
    d. All of the above

19. _____ can boost the supervisor's opportunities for career advancement.

    a. Staying single
    b. Finding the right mentor
    c. Having a few really close friends
    d. All of the above

20. The supervisor should not underestimate _____ in seeking advancement.

    a. His own abilities
    b. The surrender of ethics
    c. The unacceptable emotional burden
    d. The possibility of the loss of friends

ANSWERS

1. B., 329

2. C., 329

3. A., 330

4. D., 330

5. C., 330

6. B., 331

7. A., 332

8. B., 333

9. A., 333

10. C., 334

11. B., 334

12. C., 335

13. B., 336

14. D., 337

15. B., 337

16. D., 339

17. C., 340

18. D., 341

19. B., 342

20. A., 342

Chapter 20

DIFFERENCES IN LEADING DIFFERENT GENERATIONS: FACT OR MYTH?

SUMMARY

There are indeed differences between employees born in the 1940s and 50s and those just coming into today's workplace. Each generation's style of working and communicating can be a little different from the others. So are their expectations of their employer, their immediate supervisor, and themselves. Each group brings peculiarities as well as skills and talents to the work environment. There also may be overlapping characteristics from one generational group to another. By remaining flexible in his approach to supervising all of these people the law enforcement leader should be able to get their best from each. Patience and a sincere caring about the welfare of each subordinate, regardless of generational background, will help the police supervisor reach them. Good things should happen as a result.

QUESTIONS

1. Which of the following are considered generational groupings?

   a. Baby Boomers
   b. Generation Xers
   c. Both a and b
   d. Neither a nor b

2. Which of the following are considered generational groupings?

   a. Veterans
   b. Millennials
   c. Both a and b
   d. Neither a nor b

3. What is often considered the birthdate range for the Baby Boomers generation?

   a. 1946–1964
   b. 1922–1945
   c. 1965–1980
   d. None of the above

4. What is often considered the birthdate range for the Generation Xers?

   a. 1922–1945
   b. 1946–1964
   c. 1990–present
   d. None of the above

5. What are the Baby Boomers said to value highly?

   a. Their work lives
   b. Their work achievements
   c. Both a and b
   d. Neither a nor b

6. This group tends to believe that work comes before play.

    a. Baby Boomers
    b. Generation X
    c. Millennials
    d. None of the above

7. Overall, this generational group respects authority.

    a. Generation Y
    b. Generation X
    c. Baby Boomers
    d. All of the above

8. Members of this generational group do not necessarily accept supervisors as the "ultimate authority," and are not hesitant to ask "Why?"

    a. Veterans
    b. Baby Boomers
    c. Generation X
    d. All of the above

9. There sometimes can be _____ of generational groups' characteristics.

    a. Opposition
    b. Confusion
    c. Narrow-banding
    d. Overlapping

10. The Millennials are sometimes called _____.

    a. Baby Boomers
    b. Veterans
    c. Generation Y
    d. Generation X

11. For the supervisor, when it comes to generations of employees, relying heavily on stereotyping can prove _____.

    a. Wise
    b. Appropriate
    c. Efficient
    d. Ill-advised

12. The members of this generational group are not as dependent upon their work life for personal fulfillment as were members of some earlier generations.

    a. Generation X
    b. Baby Boomers
    c. Veterans
    d. None of the above

13. Members of this generational group often can learn most effectively from the use of interactive, technology-based instruction.

    a. Veterans
    b. Millennials
    c. Baby Boomers
    d. None of the above

14. Regardless of the generation they are a part of, all employees want to be treated with fairness and _____.

    a. Firmness
    b. Condolences
    c. Respect
    d. Stereotyping

15. Guidelines the supervisor may apply to assure relative workplace harmony include which of the following?

    a. Accommodate different learning styles
    b. Use several means of communication
    c. Recognize and respect differences
    d. All of the above

16. Guidelines the supervisor may apply to assure relative workplace harmony include which of the following?

    a. Don't show favoritism
    b. Resist dropping into stereotyping
    c. Ask for (and expect) everyone's best
    d. All of the above

17. Additional guidelines the supervisor may apply to assure relative harmony in the workplace include which of the following?

    a. Minimize the formal meetings
    b. Recognize good work
    c. Give everyone a voice
    d. All of the above

18. Additional guidelines the supervisor may apply to assure relative harmony in the workplace include which of the following?

    a. Use employees' names
    b. Emphasize the positive similarities, not how people are dissimilar
    c. Be sure deadlines are understood
    d. All of the above

19. Which is true of each generation of employees?

    a. Each generation's style of communicating can be a little different from the others.
    b. Expectations of their employer may differ.
    c. Expectations of themselves may differ.
    d. All of the above are true.

20. Patience and _____ about the welfare of each subordinate should aid the police supervisor in reaching them, regardless of their identity.

    a. Love
    b. Forgiveness
    c. Firmness
    d. Genuine caring

ANSWERS

1. C., 345

2. C., 345–346

3. A., 345

4. D., 345

5. C., 345

6. A., 345

7. C., 345

8. C., 345

9. D., 346

10. C., 346

11. D., 346

12. A., 345

13. B., 345

14. C., 347

15. D., 347

16. D., 347–348

17. D., 348–349

18. D., 341–350

19. D., 350–351

20. D., 351